Motivating the Di

Asperger Syndrome and high functioning autism: guidelines for education post 16

Hilary Dinham

Asperger Syndrome and high functioning autism: guidelines for education post 16

Published by Lifetime Careers Wiltshire, 7 Ascot Court, White Horse Business Park, Trowbridge BA14 0XA.

ISBN 1 902876 70 9

Printed by Cromwell Press, Trowbridge
Cover illustration by Russell Cobb
Text design by Ministry of Design

Motivating the Disaffected

Series editor: Dr Gerald Lombard

Asperger Syndrome and high functioning autism: guidelines for education post 16 is one of a series of six titles designed to help professionals in education and advisory work to motivate and encourage students who are disengaged from learning.

Each book provides a concise and practical guide to topics that are of particular concern to teachers and advisers.

The other titles in the series are:

The ABC Approach to Classroom Behaviour Management
Motivational Triggers
Social Competency: reading other people
Complex Specific Learning Difficulties
Staying Safe

To order copies, please contact Orca Book Services Ltd, Stanley House, 3 Fleets Lane, Poole, Dorset BH15 3AJ. Tel: 01202 665432. Fax: 01202 666219.

For further information about these and other products published by Lifetime Careers Publishing, please contact our customer services, tel: 01225 716023; email: sales@lifetime-publishing.co.uk, or www.lifetime-publishing.co.uk

Hilary Dinham, MA AFBPsS

Hilary is a freelance chartered educational psychologist. Having trained at the University of Nottingham under Professor Elizabeth Newson, Hilary worked for three London education authorities over the following 19 years. During this period she maintained an active interest in autism spectrum disorders (ASD), offering training and advising on services as well as assessing children and young people.

In 1996, Hilary began to work independently, specialising in assessments and training in ASD. Alongside this she has undertaken training for court work. She now specialises in the 14+ age group with ASD, working mainly with colleges. Hilary also offers assessment for the courts on young people with ASD who are 'looked after', young parents or alleged offenders.

This publication is aimed at those working with adolescents and young adults who have Asperger Syndrome or high functioning autism. Because it is 'pocket-sized' it cannot be all-inclusive nor offer information in depth and the reader is referred to fuller texts, organisations and websites for further information.

Acknowledgements

I would like to thank Raphael and Sarah, two students who persevered, and also the staff at Swindon and Salisbury Colleges who have worked hard to integrate students with autism spectrum disorders. Most of what is written in this booklet comes from my time working with them all between 1996 and 2002.

Thank you also to David Sherratt, a valued friend and colleague who kindly read a draft of the booklet and gave useful advice.

Hilary Dinham

Contents

Section 1
Characteristics of Asperger Syndrome and high functioning autism

Diagnostic criteria for Asperger Syndrome

There is still considerable controversy about what constitutes the criteria for diagnosis and some professionals and researchers question whether Asperger Syndrome can be defined separately from autism. In fact there is even disagreement about whether it is a syndrome or a disorder, Asperger or Asperger's!

In all instances, Asperger (pronounce it to rhyme with hamburger) Syndrome and high functioning autism are characterised by a number of impairments that pervade development and everyday living. Clusters of symptoms must be present for the diagnosis. Many of the symptoms of Asperger Syndrome and autism are found in other disorders such as specific language disorder, dyspraxia, schizophrenia, reaction to extreme trauma and attachment disorder. It is the presence of certain characteristics together and from early childhood that leads to a diagnosis of Asperger Syndrome or autism.

Diagnosis should always be by experienced, appropriately qualified personnel, preferably a team, including a paediatrician or psychiatrist, and psychologist. A thorough background history is necessary as well as interviews with the person concerned, their family and associated professionals.

The two main classification systems currently used in the UK are ICD-10 (World Health Organisation, 1992) and DSM-IV (American Psychiatric Association, 1994). They are similar in how they describe Asperger Syndrome, but not identical. It is important to realise that both classification systems ask for 'serious' and 'significant' impairments. DSM-IV is more detailed. Prominent researchers in the area, such as Christopher Gillberg and Lorna Wing have also contributed to the debate and put forward their criteria (see Wing, 1988, Attwood, 1998).

For the purpose of this publication, the 'triad of impairments' is used: this term was first coined by Lorna Wing and Judith Gould (Wing, 1988, but see also Wing, 1996) and it is most useful for educationalists. Again it is important to realise that each impairment may differ in level of severity and how it is manifested. Those with Asperger Syndrome or autism are people first: people with personalities, histories and experiences that will affect how they deal with the world. Their Asperger Syndrome or autism provides an additional 'layer' through which they have to understand the world around them.

The focus in this publication will be on students who are of at least average intellectual ability. Whether they have high functioning autism or Asperger Syndrome, the impairments will be similar and interventions are to a large extent similar for both groups. Richard Exley, who has Asperger Syndrome, once told me that he considers the difference between the two is that those with autism do not wish to socialise, those with Asperger Syndrome do, but do not know how. Whether or not this is so, each student is an individual with his or her own personality, struggling with adolescence and developing identity, and these factors need to be considered as well as the Asperger Syndrome or high functioning autism. Both come under the heading of autism spectrum disorders (ASD), a term used in this publication alongside high functioning autism and Asperger Syndrome.

The triad of impairments

- an impairment in communication skills

- an impairment in social interaction skills

- an impairment in flexible thought and behaviour.

Those with autism spectrum disorders may also be clumsy and may show challenging behaviour. *It is essential to remember that these are impairments not deficits and that each student displays the characteristics of the disorder in different ways.* For example, not all able students with autism spectrum disorder react badly to change, some do. Not all these students show difficult behaviour.

Impairment in communication

Why *do* we communicate? There are many reasons, mostly social, although we also need to obtain our basic needs and to gain information about our environment. The ways we communicate include:

- greeting

- asking

- instructing

- stating

- inviting comment, drawing attention to something

- offering

- teasing or joking

- arguing.

Communication, two-way interaction, begins when babies are a few hours old. With the use of close eye contact, movements of the body, stilling of the body and vocalisation, communication is set up between baby and carers. By six to eight weeks the baby has learned to smile and uses this to good effect to initiate and prolong interaction with carers. Adults modify their language and their intonation, they talk about the here and now. They imitate the baby's expression and sounds and make playful faces. As the baby develops he or she begins to look about, inviting comment from adults.

However, when the child with autism spectrum disorder is developing, these early signals and interactions rarely occur. The child may not be interested in faces or in interacting. The consequent disturbance in the interaction can affect how the parent continues to react to the baby. The subtle messages are different. The baby may not respond normally in imitating sounds. The baby may cry out and the mother may misinterpret this as a wish for the preceding act to stop when the baby's intention was otherwise. As the child grows, the adults' expectations naturally change: they think about how old the child is and use language accordingly. The situation is made more complex when the child with autism is relatively able and uses echolalic ('echoing' what has been heard without fully comprehending) language or perhaps recites long passages from books or the television adverts. This may cause adults to think the child is more able to communicate than he or she actually is.

In summary, the child with autism will not be taking part in many of the ways of communicating mentioned above and may have missed out on many of the early stages in interaction.

By adolescence, the more able person with autism spectrum disorder will probably have a good range of vocabulary and be able to cope with at least the first four of the communication skills mentioned above. Assessment of these skills and others will be essential to enable tutors and support staff to interact effectively with the student and enable further development of communication skills.

Impairments in communication may be manifested as follows:

- may express self well but in formal or pedantic manner

- may lack expression and talk in monotone

- may appear to talk at people rather than with them

- may be having problems in interpreting and using non-verbal language (gesture, facial expressions, body language)

- may have problems comprehending subtle or complex language

- language is usually interpreted literally and there may be little or no understanding of metaphor or idiom

- students with ASD often have difficulty in switching attention from one modality to another and from one type of task to another.

What other factors do we need to consider before embarking on intervention?

Attention and listening skills are crucial and we need to understand how these develop if our intervention programme is to be successful. By adolescence we expect students to take in instructions while occupied on another task, shift from instruction to task, and accept advice from others to help in completion of a task. The tutor may use just language to gain attention at a distance. It is therefore important to assess the student's level of attention in different contexts: one to one, a small group, a large group or outside the classroom. It may be that the tutor will need to be physically closer to the student to gain full attention and understanding, the student may have to stop and look to assimilate instructions. While students may appear to take in instructions, it is worth checking for full comprehension and recall of the instructions.

Another important factor is that of *motivation*. What is in it for the student? Why should he or she want to communicate? Carefully assessing the student's interests, favourite foods, activities, etc as well as those not tolerated, will be important to ensure motivation.

Impairment in social interaction skills

These skills become more important as the young person with autism spectrum disorder reaches adolescence. Peers expect some social conformity, a knowledge of what is currently 'cool'. They are more questioning and discussions can go into more depth. There is the expectation by adults that the young person will be able to cope with certain social situations: travel by public transport, shopping, dealing with everyday difficulties, getting around college or university, dealing with the canteen and social life. All of the above may be profoundly difficult for the adolescent with autism spectrum disorder (ASD), even with high intellectual ability. In fact, good cognitive skills often make the situation more complex as the young person may question some of the social situations and peers, perhaps to the point of alienating him or herself.

On the other hand, many young people with high functioning autism or Asperger Syndrome have learned very appropriate ways of dealing with social situations, albeit at a superficial level. They may be excellent at greeting, very polite and helpful and know the appropriate behaviour for queues, and other common social processes. They are still likely to have significant problems beyond this superficial level. This is especially true in new situations or when they are presented with conflict.

In social contexts all the impairments contribute to make them uncomfortable situations where the usual integration of skills does not occur.

In summary, this impairment may be expressed by students with high functioning autism and Asperger Syndrome in the following ways:

- may be socially isolated (may or may not like this state)

- may lack spontaneity in social interaction, approaches may appear 'rehearsed' or formal

- may make inappropriate social approaches (too close, no discrimination of strangers versus family)

- difficulties in perceiving social cues (irritation, lack of interest, mocking)

- difficulty in sustaining social interaction after greetings

- may not know how to end social interaction

- in class, may not have skills to intervene with point of view in a group discussion. May then bring in viewpoint well after that topic has been passed

- students with high functioning autism and Asperger Syndrome are generally very anxious and keen to please and to be accepted. With appropriate support most can manage their social impairment and be rewarding members of the course.

Impairment in flexibility of thought, social imagination, resistance to change

In some texts it mentions that those with high functioning autism and Asperger Syndrome have a lack of imagination. It is more a lack of flexibility and a lack of seeing others' viewpoints. Students with high functioning autism and Asperger Syndrome often prefer factual material as it is 'safer'. However, those with ASD *can* write vividly, paint creatively, act on stage convincingly and show imagination in activities. Do not assume anything!

In early childhood, this impairment may not be as evident as the impairments in communication and social skills. It is in secondary school and after that more abstract thought is expected, the National Curriculum and GCSE Syllabuses expect older students to compare and contrast, to estimate, question and critically analyse to some extent. In further and higher education these skills are essential and it is then that this impairment is often most evident.

In summary, this impairment is shown in some or all of the following ways:

- may have problems transferring skills from one setting to another

- may not be able to plan ahead in problem solving, course work, etc

- may lack skills in organisation

- written work may not 'flow' and may go from one subject to another as student does not understand that the reader cannot follow his or her train of thought

- limited ability to see others' viewpoints and contrast views

- difficulties in interpreting emotions (own and others)

- may lack empathy (e.g. may laugh at someone's despair or sadness through lack of understanding of the cues)

- may assume you know what he or she is thinking or feeling (egocentric view)

- may lack inhibition; may be impulsive

- sense of humour often limited to slapstick, or certain types of jokes will probably be greeted with 'over the top' laughter by the student

- seems to lack 'common sense' of age group

- may have obsessions about tidying or having possessions in certain places

- may have all absorbing interests connected with transport systems or maps

- may need to adhere strictly to routines and rules; may find change in these unsettling

- rigidity about following rules and instructions may make the student dismissive or derogatory about classmates who have not followed the rules or appear not to have persevered n an activity.

Motor clumsiness

Not always present and there are students with Asperger Syndrome who are agile with excellent coordination skills. Those that suffer from motor clumsiness will show this in:

- awkward gait

- problems in dealing with sequences, especially handwriting

- problems in organising self, getting him or herself to college, having the right materials, finding the way round college, being in the right place at the right time

- problems in organising self to start, order and complete written work

- problems with timing and pace.

(Resources on study skills and those written for students with specific learning difficulties, dyspraxia or dyslexia may be useful here for ideas on intervention.)

As a result of the above impairments, there are effects in many areas of functioning. Donna Williams (1996, see also Harrison, 1998), an able adult with ASD, talks of difficulties with connections, tolerance and control.

Connections

- attention: distracted by detail (pattern of ceiling tiles, lines on floor)

- perception: processing the parts not seeing the whole unless presented by another (e.g. a model or example of what is expected)

- sensory integration: firing on one channel (listening so not seeing, speaking so not thinking)

- information processing: information accumulated but no context, need external trigger to help.

Tolerance

- sensory hypersensitivity: feeling bombarded with smells, noise, sights

- emotional hypersensitivity: intense unpredictable emotions, cannot name and may be overwhelmed by them

- fear of exposure, wanting to avoid others, assume another voice to distance from emotions and insecurity associated with own voice and self.

Control

- compulsion to do things triggered by others' acts/speech, when may not wish to

- obsession with all absorbing interests, lines, patterns may prevent other productive activity or even reaching places

- anxiety: unreasonable fear about anything in environment, may fiddle and twiddle or use repetitive speech to calm self.

(Based on Harrison, 1998)

Section 2
Preparation for college entry and courses

Transition from school or other educational establishment

This section offers suggestions for those in colleges and universitites who co-ordinate the entry of students with special needs.

- Ensure good regular links with Connexions Personal Advisers/careers advisers to gain information on possible students for the following academic year.

- Ideally information is needed in year 10 so taster sessions can be organised for year 11.

- These should be set up following receipt of relevant information and meeting with key people including parents or carers.

- The students' progress in taster sessions should be reviewed before college acceptance for the autumn.

- Has the student applied for Disabled Students' Allowance? Is this a possibility? Any psychological reports needed to back applications for allowances or support should be organised in year 11, as there is often a long wait.

- When the student has a Statement of Special Educational Needs (SEN), ask when the Annual Review is and try to attend in year 11 at least.

- Ask for Statement of SEN, Transitional Review report, last Individual Educational Plan.

- Complete checklist (see Appendix 1). You can download a fuller specific checklist (The Australian Scale for Asperger Syndrome) from www.tonyattwood.com that may be helpful obtaining full information from schools.

Before the course begins

- Ensure the enrolment forms have a section for disabilities and give 'autism spectrum disorders' as one of the examples. Although many students will have been identified through taster sessions, some may have moved in from elsewhere or come from mainstream schools so ask if there are any reports, reviews or a Statement of Special Educational Needs. If not, ask for permission to contact the last establishment to gain information on the areas of impairment and behaviour, strategies etc (see checklist in Appendix 1).

- Is the course appropriate for the student's skills, ability level and the characteristics of autism shown?

- Check if student has Disabled Students' Allowance (see above).

- Provide clear maps of campus, details of contact personnel or key worker and counsellor (names, location, phone number, days and hours available).

- Ask permission to have contact with parents or carers.

- Obtain contact details of GP and gain permission to have contact if there are ever any health issues during the course.

- If support in class is required, organise it as soon as possible, preferably before the student begins the full course.

- Consider plan for induction of student: where possible this should be in the term before entry, and ensure this is made clear to student.

- Induction should include being taken around to key locations and meeting key people and this should not be rushed, giving time for questions or for the student to make notes if needed.

- Go through 'ground rules' with student: include expectations for attendance, punctuality, behaviour, note taking, assignment writing (including quality expected). These should be written in simple clear language and gone through with the student, a copy each and signed. These can then be referred to during the course as necessary.

Access to lectures and courses

- Ensure there is individual space for students to allow those with autism spectrum disorders their own 'corner'.

- It has been found useful for secondary schools and colleges to have a quiet room where students with autism spectrum disorders can go. This may be a small room next to the library or part of the learning support department. There should be a member of staff nearby and access to a telephone in case of extreme distress or need.

- Have classroom rules about level of noise and movement and stick to them.

- Encourage the student to carry a brightly coloured notebook or other device in which to note messages, information, dates etc when around college or in the classroom.

Access to leisure facilities

- Take the student to see the library, canteen and any leisure facilities. Students with ASD may require more than one visit and may prefer to be shown alone or in a small group rather than with all the course group.

- Ask the student if he or she is uncomfortable in any of the places and why. Ask the student if there are any ways in which the facilities would make it easier for the student to go there and see if modifications are feasible.

- Does the college have a canteen where it is easy to draw up a chair or are there benches (making it harder to join a group sitting there)?

- Ensure canteen and library staff know the student has ASD and are aware of what effects this may have in their context.

- Some canteens echo or are very loud and it may help the student to be encouraged to have early or late lunch and to sit near the door. Consider having some system to lower the noise level for all students' and staff comfort.

Contingency plans and leaving college

- Contingency plans are important in case the student cannot cope with part of the course or it is clear that the course is somehow inappropriate.

- It is also important to offer a planning meeting near the end of a student's time at college or university where a handover to adult services, another establishment or transition to work can be discussed. Connexions/careers services can again be involved here and it is valuable to involve parents too. This is where links with health and social services will be useful.

Section 3
Hints for college or university staff

Planning and preparation are the keys to ensuring students with Asperger Syndrome or high functioning autism have full access to courses. This is, of course, true for all students, but because the impairments of autism spectrum disorders can have such devastating effects in new situations, good preparation is essential. Some of the suggestions have been mentioned in previous sections but they are important enough to be repeated here.

Preliminary planning

- Has the Learning Support Manager or coordinator for autism spectrum disorders completed a checklist? (See Appendix 1.)

- Is the course a relevant and appropriate one for the student?

- Ensure you are aware of the characteristics of Asperger Syndrome and possible effects in your area.

- Ensure any reports from previous educational establishment have been read.

- Ensure that the learning support staff in your establishment know about the student and can offer support with a member of staff or a room, as necessary.

- Set up an Individual Progress Plan (see Appendix 2) with the student, parents/carers, learning support staff, other tutors as relevant. This may seem time consuming but the investment of time at the start will be well worth it.

- Carry out a 'risk assessment' of the student's behaviour in different contexts. (See also under 'Behaviour' later in this section.)

- Students may be able to read fluently but it is worth checking the level of comprehension as this is sometimes much lower than reading accuracy skill.

Ideas to facilitate learning

Structure

Structure is known to be a key feature in the learning environment of students with ASD. This means considering the layout of the classroom and ensuring it is the same each time the student has to use the room; perhaps he or she can choose a particular place to sit. There will also need to be structure in the timetable, to ensure the student knows when and where lessons take place. The student should have a copy of this schedule. There should also be structure in how the student approaches activities. Structure of this kind is usual in many schools but less common in colleges and universities. However, having a basic environmental structure can ease anxiety and thus allow the student to focus on comprehension of what is being shared or taught. It can help independence in learning and promote calm, focused behaviour.

Whether it is a lesson, a workshop or work experience, remember the student with ASD will need to be able to answer for himself or herself:

- What do I have to do here?

- What materials do I need for the task?

- How much do I have to do?

- How will I know when I have finished?

- What will the finished product look like?

- How do I know what to do next?

- What do I do if I do not understand or I am stuck?

Class environment

- Ensure the environment is physically safe with the same layout each lesson.

- Try to offer a calm environment.

- Try to give physical space.

- Avoid forcing physical proximity, crowded situations.

- Discuss with student to see if noise or other sensory experiences are upsetting.

- Where possible talk to the student before courses to discover where he or she is most comfortable in the room. This is often facing or near the door. Over time help the student to accept other positions but gently and with support.

- Learn about triggers that can unsettle the student and try to avoid these.

- Group work may be problematic. Consider working in pairs or allowing individual work.

Approach

- Be consistent with the timetable; changes will unsettle the student with ASD.

- Ensure activities are meaningful for the student.

- Break up work into small steps wherever possible; have these written down so the student has a copy and can check them.

- Be consistent in approach.

- Where possible, offer continuity in terms of those working with the student (especially support staff).

- Offer more positive reinforcement for appropriate communication and behaviour than would normally be the case.

- Use the student's interests as creatively as you can to gain the student's motivation. You can then move from this to other areas.

- Ensure transitions in topic and session are well-managed with thorough explanation.

- Decide with colleagues which behaviour to accept or ignore, and that which you will all try to modify or not accept.

- Check texts such as Cumine, Leach and Stevenson (1998) for 'top tips' that may be relevant to you.

- Many students with Asperger Syndrome, like those with dyspraxia, benefit from 'one made earlier': they need to see and understand what they are working towards and so a model or visual example can be very helpful.

- Switching from one topic to another, one modality to another may be difficult for the student, check for this and consider ways of facilitating this.

- Do not take comments or misbehaviour personally: students with ASD are seldom manipulative although they can appear blunt and tactless. remember their honesty has a positive side too.

Communication hints

- Simplify your language and use short sentences when explaining or instructing.

- Avoid subtle 'polite' language as it may confuse or be literally interpreted (*'Would you like to start work now?'*, *'Your voice is very loud'*). In these examples you infer the action you expect and the student with ASD may not pick this up.

- Give one instruction at a time.

- If addressing the student, start with his or her name to gain attention.

- Use variation in tone and pitch to keep attention.

- Keep gestures and facial expressions clear.

- Do not assume that the student will understand your non-verbal language and feelings.

- When you are addressing the whole group, ensure you make it clear that the student is included. Some students with Asperger Syndrome or autism will not realise you are including them unless you are looking at them or have stated before you begin that you wish everyone to listen, as whatever follows is for everyone.

- Encourage eye contact when the student is talking to you; explain it is all right to look away or down sometimes when he or she is explaining (as we all do).

- Try to accept the student's attempts to communicate, however simple.

- Set up situations that will encourage the student to communicate appropriately.

- Give the student time to respond.

- Listening skills may appear limited: check as may be distraction, lack of comprehension, anxiety.

- Because of distraction of detail in some pictures, activities etc the student may lose concentration: check for this and modify if possible.

- Check for full understanding. Avoid closed questions where yes/no are the answers, for checking comprehension ask 'what' and 'how' type questions. Try *'What will you do first in this task?'* and check at regular intervals.

- Individual prompts may be necessary, as the student may not know what to do next or how to tell you the task is finished.

- Where necessary, give extra visual clues (diagrams, flow charts, pictures) to help the student understand.

- Give a written, brief (bullet-pointed) overview of the lesson structure with oral back up.

Coursework

- Start where the students are, not where you think they should be.

- Decide on priorities for learning for students with ASD.

- These students may lack the expected level of study skills, so consider how help and support may be offered.

- Self-directed and incidental learning can be difficult for such students, especially if their disorder has only recently been diagnosed and appropriate intervention was not implemented in school. Realise you will have to teach the student. Do not expect generalisation: if it occurs, celebrate as a major step.

- Whatever is taught, it will be followed up by other tutors, support staff and maybe by those living with the student to ensure generalisation.

- Always try to involve the student in any special programme, plan or targets as they have a right to be consulted.

- Always indicate what should be done rather than what should not be done.

- Try to have written back up for instructions – short, concise and numbered so steps are clear.

- If you are involved in a communications or literacy course, consider using one of the books written by a young person with Asperger Syndrome. Those by Claire Sainsbury and Luke Jackson have been well reviewed in the national press and both have content that would lead to discussion and debate in class. The National Autistic Society (NAS) Publications Catalogue has a list of some other personal accounts. The reading level should be well within the reach of able students with ASD.

- Take account of rigidity of thinking in oral and written work: if this is an issue, learning support staff should be involved to try and extend the student's ideas and writing a little further.

- Literal thinking and language may also be an issue in discussion, watching film/video, using texts: allow for this.

- Listening and then taking notes can be extremely difficult as the student will wish to write verbatim. Support staff intervention may be needed here.

- Consider a written sheet with key phrases or even most of the text and ask the student to listen and follow on the written sheet. Ask students in the group for keywords and phrases that are important as those with specific literacy difficulties may also find this process hard.

- For written work expected in the lesson, try giving a bullet pointed outline in sequence to help the student.

Written work

- A written piece may require input, to provide ideas on the order in which ideas should appear, as well as what to include. For commonly used sequences, try a template that the student can refer to but ensure he or she is very clear about how to use this before being left to work independently.

- Some students may not wish to do assignments in certain areas or outside their own area of interest. It is therefore important that 'ground rules' are set up at the start of the course where it is explained that the tutor sets the titles and the student should adhere to these in order to achieve accreditation. The ground rule can then be referred to before each assignment as necessary.

- Students with Asperger Syndrome may have difficulties with completing work by the deadline. Give stepped deadlines and check they have been met (plan by 4th, introduction by 8th etc).

- Comprehension, literal understanding, writing from the imagination may all cause problems. Again, additional support to explain and take over one task (such as scribing) to enable the student to focus fully on one area may be useful.

- Written work can be repetitive in vocabulary used, so some work on synonyms can be helpful.

- Students may not be able to keep to the subject and sequence when writing and may flit from one thing to another. Go through work with the student and try to discover the thinking behind the flitting, as there may be some logic to it or some creative idea that has not been conveyed. Act as scribe when this is done, grouping ideas. Always praise where you can and emphasise that you want to learn fully what is being conveyed to ensure marking is fair.

- Ensure there is a written plan of headings, that the student understands what to do, where to find resources and when it has to be handed in. Ensure the student understands the main idea or theme (this may be difficult). Prompt before hand-in date.

- Creative thinking can be a difficulty. On the other hand, lack of inhibition means many able students with autism spectrum disorders have zany and truly creative ideas and these can be encouraged and harnessed within the context of the course.

- Referring to others' research or views and critically appraising them can be extremely difficult for even the most able student with ASD. The student will need help extracting relevant information from others' work and then perhaps tabulating this to look at similarities and differences. The student can then be encouraged to give his or her views.

- For students working on a project or thesis, it would be helpful to make it contemporary if possible. Interviews with people in the field, gaining their views on a question or topic can provide some useful quotes and be more meaningful for the student than citing 'dead' text or internet information.

- Students with ASD often demonstrate good attention to detail and excellent memory: use them!

Specific subject areas: possible difficulties

Mathematics

- Estimation and more abstract topics such as algebra may cause difficulties. Written problems can cause difficulties because of the language and sequence. Additional support and explanation may be required in these areas.

Humanities

- Student may not fully comprehend in areas where he or she has no experience, such as historical times, other cultures and religions. These may be misunderstood or dismissed.

Science

- In the first instance, forming hypotheses can be difficult. Actual experiments may be carried out with ease but recording them accurately in sequence can be hard – *'I know what happened so why don't you?'*

Social interaction

- Check whether the student wishes to mix or socialise: he or she may not.

- Explain if student is too close and that when talking with you and other staff he or she should stand 'this' distance away and discreetly demonstrate.

- The student with ASD may stand there when you have given non-verbal cues that the interview or conversation is over: try asking where student should be next and then stating he or she should now go there.

- Consider a buddy system to support student in social contexts. Try to share this amongst two or three students or ensure they take turns as this role can be wearing. The 'buddies' will need support and a regular time to offload, obtain ideas, feedback. The system by which this is managed needs to be organised sensitively, involving the student as much as possible.

- Students may not be happy with the term 'buddy' in which case they can determine the term to be used. One student chose 'nudger' for the students who reminded him about inappropriate behaviour.

- Some colleges are now realising that it is worthwhile to run their own social skills workshops, as there is little support in the community. There are published texts that may help here (e.g. *Talkabout* by Alex Kelly, *The Social Skills Handbook* by Hutchings, Comins and Offiler, both available through Smallwood Publishing). It is also worth contacting the National Autistic

Society and OAASIS for up to date information on their courses or workshops. (See 'Useful organisations' for details.)

- It is important to include work on what a friend is or is not. For example, students with ASD can view helpful professionals as 'friends' and then become angry or distressed when the professional does not wish to go out on a date or be phoned at home in the evening. Politeness does not always equal acceptance, and students need to learn some key questions to ask others and themselves. In these respects the social skills programme has to be more detailed and look at basic premises, which is why many published programmes are only suitable as a basis and need to be further developed for use with students who have ASD.

- Role play and use of video can also be useful. Companies such as Incentive Plus have useful material in this area.

- Consider using Social Stories, a method pioneered by Carol Gray. Many of the publications give examples for children, but check the website www.thegraycenter.org for details. Winslow distribute *Social Skills Stories* by Anne Marie Johnson and Jackie Susnik and *More Social Skills Stories* by Anne Marie Johnson.

- Out in the community, or on a work placement, it may be helpful to have some of the 'business cards' produced by the National Autistic Society that explain about the holder having an autism spectrum disorder.

- Social groups: some areas run these for young adults with Asperger Syndrome. They are not an easy option and require commitment and regular work with the young adults concerned. NAS regional officers have set these up in collaboration with local communities. It may be worth considering if you have several young adults in your establishment who would benefit from organised after-college contact. Check the website www.nas.org.uk or contact them for further details.

Although those with ASD may have problems interpreting emotions or showing their own appropriately, they do have feelings and can sympathise.

It is the expression of these that causes difficulties. Consider doing some work on this with programmes from companies such as Incentive Plus (see under References) or consider software such as *Emotion Trainer* which is an interactive CD-ROM that aims to improve the user's understanding of emotions and aid social skills.

Mind Reading is another interactive piece of software that explains a wide range of emotions and there are also quizzes to test emotion recognition. See under the References section for details of both programs.

Help in dealing with rigidity of thought, repetitive behaviour, etc

- Prepare the student for changes in routine, room, staff, new students joining the course.

- Encourage student to try new locations, new partners for working together, but do this within the student's individual plan targets and with support staff assistance as necessary.

- Prepare work in small structured steps.

- Offer checklist of regular activity and encourage independence in checking this during the activity.

- Ensure student knows what is expected.

- Reward non-interruption or appropriate contribution.

- Encourage choices and decision-making: if this is stressful, make the activity or choice simpler.

- Help with the organisation of written assignments: see section on written work for suggestions.

- If the student has a need to talk incessantly about particular topics, arrange a plan where you explain it is all right to talk about these things sometimes and this is going to be a certain time each day with a certain person. Outside of these times, the student has to 'keep it in'.

- If the student talks about inappropriate topics or uses inappropriate words (sexual matters, rows at home, swear words, certain jokes) explain that these subjects are for quiet talk with friends or family only. Explain focus must be on the task. These topics are not for work sessions.

- If the student uses an argument or phrase repeatedly and cannot seem to move on, there is likely to be increased agitation too: acknowledge that there is clearly something upsetting the student and decide when this can be discussed and then attempt to move the lesson on.

- Rigidity arises from anxiety about not being in control. Sudden rages or panic attacks are usually due to anxiety about not understanding or someone intruding on the student's privacy (e.g. looking at his or her books or work). To deal with this use strategies known to be successful with that student (different room, different member of staff, asking student to write down what is wrong, do not expect or ask for eye contact or physical contact during these times, in fact avoid both). Keep voice calm, use simple language and repeat calmly that student is safe and OK, keep speech to a minimum (see also paragraghs below on behaviour).

- Try to find alternatives for strange mannerisms, need to twiddle, swear etc. For example, a small item can be kept in the pocket for twiddling when anxious. Worry beads may help. Talk to the student about the behaviour, indicating you want him or her to be part of the course but the behaviour is affecting others' progress so something needs to change. Explain that the behaviour is for certain places like home, own room, etc.

- Use any obsessive tidying behaviour in a constructive way.

- To gradually modify obsessions or adherence to routines, try 'graded change' (see Howlin, 1997, chapter 5 for details and good advice).

Behaviour

Not all students with ASD show challenging or inappropriate behaviour. It is well worth carrying out a risk assessment for behaviour at the start of a student's course so that difficulties are known about and can be addressed.

Students with ASD are also dealing with adolescence and the development of self-identity and worth. It is more of a challenge for them to manage this life transition with their cluster of impairments and therefore high levels of tolerance and understanding are recommended.

Outbursts are usually due to a lack of understanding, anxiety over change or proximity of another student, teasing, not understanding the social situation or not having a repertoire of reactions to deal with specific situations. The student may not have the communication skills to repair the situation and then panic. The student may want something or someone to stop whatever it is that is happening and may shout, push or threaten. The threat may be overdone as in threatening to blow the person up (one extremely able student told the author he had a bomb in his bedroom so she had to watch out).

- Try to assess what function the challenging behaviour serves. Is it escape or avoidance? Is it because of unpleasant sensory stimuli? Is it to gain a preferred activity? Has another student invaded this student's personal space or touched possessions without permission?

- Try to 'rewind' and discover what triggered the outburst as it may be something that can easily be modified or dealt with (e.g. a phrase taken literally that caused fear or reluctance).

- Because of the impairments characteristic of ASD, the student may not be able to distinguish between minor incidents and serious ones.

- It is also worth remembering that many people with ASD do not feel pain in the same way as others and may not recognise danger.

- Positive reinforcement can be effective with the right incentives and in limited situations. However, as generalisation is usually a problem, do not expect behaviour modification techniques to work outside the specific situation in which you are using them.

- It may help for a trusted member of staff to sit with the student and work out a series of things that the student should do when upset or stressed. This can include deep breathing, twiddling with favourite object in pocket, going to the quiet room, and going to a named support worker. Have the steps wordprocessed and put or a business card or postcard, preferably coloured and laminated so the student can put it in a pocket or wallet for easy access. If a tutor sees a student becoming anxious he or she can then prompt, 'check your card' in a discreet manner.

- Every educational establishment should have a policy on challenging behaviour and critical incidents. One suggestion is to incorporate into this some ideas for dealing with students with ASD who have outbursts.

- Check texts by Howlin (1997), Attwood (1998), Smith Myles and Southwick (1999) and those by Clements and Zarkowska (2000) on behaviour for further detailed advice in this area.

- Consider offering regular sessions on relaxation techniques so these can be used when students are near 'trigger points' or have had an angry outburst.

Some ideas to consider in the face of rage or a panic attack:

- avoid sudden movements

- maintain safe distance

- keep hands low

- avoid touch

- avoid asking student to look at you

- try to remain calm, using a firm quiet voice

- use very simple direct language

- try to convey student is safe and secure

- consider different room for student

- consider sending other students elsewhere

- consider asking another adult trusted by the student to come and deal with situation

- evaluate for any physical injury.

Sexuality and sexual issues

If the checklist (see Appendix 1) has been fully completed you will have a good idea of any problems in this area at the start of the course. Keep in mind the triad of impairments and consider how the student may have difficulties with sexual language, jokes, relationships, etc as well as knowledge. If the student has been diagnosed at an earlier stage and intervention has been in place, there may be fewer difficulties. If there are problems consult parents/carers and involve them in helping the student, having gained permission of course.

Some areas on which some sessions may be required:

- personal space

- who and where to touch, whose hand is shaken on greeting, who is hugged and kissed

- how to dress in public/private, issues of modesty (taking fashion, age and culture into account)

- respecting others' needs for privacy

- why there are different toilets, making sure the student only uses the appropriate ones

- socially acceptable names for parts of the body

- personal hygiene, menstruation

- masturbation: where and when acceptable

- how to comment on others' appearance

- dealing with sexual feelings

- how to convey interest or lack of it

- factual information on contraception, sexually transmitted diseases, pregnancy etc

- internet relationships, taking care

- dealing with approaches in public.

Look at material on the impairments and remember to keep your language direct, as concrete as possible and be consistent. Avoid euphemisms.

Many of these topics can also be addressed in social skills workshops.

There are published programmes in this area. Those for people with learning disabilities may not take account of the student's intellectual ability or impairments and may have to be adapted.

Check the NAS and OAASIS for courses in this area for staff, also check local community health teams. Try a search on a good search engine on the internet and obtain information from reputable websites (see end of publication for details).

Read the following articles from Good Autism Practice, April 1999:
Cathy Hobbs: *Sex education for adults with autism*, pages 45–53
Tula Tew: *Sexuality and adults with autism: issues and strategies*, pages 55–60.

Signs for concern

Adolescents with Asperger Syndrome or autism are more prone to mental health problems than the general population. They may develop extreme anxiety, depression, low moods or episodes of psychiatric disorder. It is rarely possible to predict whether or how a student may suffer from depression or other mental illness. Signs to look out for are the same as in any student:

- evident and sudden changes in behaviour

- significant increase or decrease in activity

- frequent low moods and appearing depressed

- significant tiredness

- significant weight loss

- mentions hearing voices when no one is there, seeing things that are not there.

Check if the student has recently started or stopped medication as this may affect behaviour. If you are concerned then use college/university procedures for involving the student and alerting appropriate medical personnel. Do not delay. Ensure there are opportunities for the student to talk and share feelings and thoughts. Ask if you can take notes and explain that, with the student's permission, these can be used to help. Also note down any advice given. This is one reason why it is useful to have the name of the student's GP/psychiatrist and permission to contact them.

Section 4
Spreading the word

Training of staff

Because of the relatively high incidence of autism spectrum disorders, it is highly recommended that your establishment has at least a half-day session of awareness training. This should include library, reception, support *and* canteen staff. This is because the main impairment that will be manifested is that of social interaction and the students may have difficulties anywhere in college or university.

Learning support staff and those tutors most likely to have students with autism spectrum disorders (e.g. IT Entry Level courses) should have more specific and in-depth training with follow-up workshops on a termly basis to share any problems.

- Asperger Initiative offer training sessions: Tel: 01424 439691 or email: admin@caretraining.com

- David Moat offers training in social integration skills. Tel: 01206 525980 or email: david.moat@ntlworld.com

One idea is for staff to develop good practice guidelines as part of their training. These can then be shared with colleagues and updated every year as different staff take part in training. The guidelines could include many of the aspects mentioned in this booklet but can be made specific to the educational establishment concerned.

It is also useful to have two or three named staff who can be consulted regarding autism spectrum disorders. These staff should have more specific training, e.g. in social skills, sexuality and also have access to key texts in the area (see References).

Some colleges now have designated staff who coordinate provision for students with autism spectrum disorders. This is highly recommended and has led to successful inclusion of many students with ASD.

A small library of key texts is highly recommended, for storage in the learning support area. It is well worth having two or more copies of favoured books.

Explaining to other students

The National Autistic Society (NAS) publishes information leaflets, including *'What is Asperger Syndrome?'* These may be useful for a group.

If the student is in a course where few, if any, others have special needs or a disability, it is advisable to consider explaining about Asperger Syndrome or autism and the effects. First, consult the student and gain permission for this. Ask whether the student wants to be present: it is preferable for them not to be.

In a group of students there will always be those who are vulnerable or perhaps have had academic or family problems. These students may be very sympathetic or it may actually bring out their vulnerability when having to relate to someone with Asperger Syndrome. This needs to be considered when providing this information.

Ensure that the person explaining to the students has a wide knowledge of the area and can handle all questions and emotions that may be shared.

Make it simple and involve the students in the discussion. Using an unusual foreign language can give the students a feel of what it is like not to comprehend. Ask the students to go into small groups and to chat about their last good night out. Then ask them to do it but looking down so there is no eye contact or nonverbal language to help. This gives a feel of what it is like to communicate without knowledge and understanding of gestures, etc. Most students have travelled abroad and there will be some who have experienced different cultures and can give anecdotes about misunderstandings. Use these too. This can lead to discussion about how the characteristics of HASD may affect a student coming into college, both socially and academically.

Use a story or autobiography to aid discussion. The books by Claire Sainsbury and Luke Johnson could be used, or a story such as *Hangman* by the popular young people's author, Julia Jarman (Anderson Press) which is about how we treat people who are different. Although it is not made explicit, the main character seems to have Asperger Syndrome.

Explain there are several examples of famous people who may have had ASD: Andy Warhol, Albert Einstein and Isaac Newton are amongst those said to have had characteristics of ASD.

How can the group help the student? Introduce the idea of the buddy system and ask if anyone would help, explain you wish to share this among two or three students and meet regularly to ensure all is well. Students may not volunteer in the session but prompt for them to approach you at a later time.

Explain that the anxieties they all have in social situations are magnified a hundred fold for the student with ASD and they should be mindful of this in the canteen and when arranging outings. You can advise (having consulted the student and parents/carers) about whether the student is likely to want to socialise or would rather be left alone. Students can still ask if help is needed etc but should not feel personally affronted if the student with ASD tells them to go away.

Work placements and visits

- Have a leaflet or 'business card' (from the NAS) ready to ease situations.

- Write a 'CV' with the student that covers some of the interests, strengths and areas about which some support or understanding may be needed.

- Prepare some guidelines to advise the student's supervisor and work colleagues.

- Role play interviews and other common situations with the student.

- Jessica Kingsley publish two books in this area: Steve Leach's *A supported Employment Workbook* and Roger Meyer's *Asperger Syndrome Employment Workbook*. There is also *Access and Inclusion: for children with autism spectrum disorders* by Matthew Hesmondhalgh and Christine Breakey (Jessica Kingsley). Although this focuses on secondary provision there is also discussion about work placements and further education. The NAS distribute this and Roger Meyer's book.

Concessions and strategies for examinations

- Check to see if student had concessions for GCSEs or SATs and how successful these were.

- Consider: extra time, a distraction free room, someone to read the paper with the student, to scribe or to prompt the student to move on to another question.

- Allow the student to see the room in advance.

- See if possible for student to sit in a preferred position: consult the student for this, do not assume.

- Consider 'mocks' and rehearsals.

- Examination papers have a language all of their own! Many students with Asperger Syndrome find it difficult to fill in the front page accurately and then to select the correct questions from various sections. It is therefore important to rehearse examinations and check to what degree the student may require support. The student may just need a prompt to move on to the next question as another difficulty is judging organisation of time.

- Some students may require interpretation of the question to ensure they know exactly what is required. Examination boards may require a psychological report to support this degree of intervention in examinations. Ensure this is sought at least a term in advance of when required.

- With the student, draw up a revision timetable and have a support member of staff check on progress as the weeks go by.

- Check all notes are available and accurate and consider revision guides.

- Ensure the student has written notice of the day, time and duration of the exam and arrange a prompt phone call the night before or early morning on the day to ensure the student attends.

Care for staff

Working with those who have ASD can produce feelings of helplessness, frustration, inadequacy, irritation and fatigue. Of course, many students with ASD give a positive contribution to the course and there are rewarding times too as students produce creative uninhibited ideas and show delight in their own progress and success, for example. However it is important to support staff with regular meetings, and known procedures for offloading or debriefing. All staff must have a chance to discuss their own feelings and have support. This is essential after any temper outburst or incidence of aggression. This type of support should be written into the college's critical incident plan and may involve the college counsellor or local health/social services or relevant voluntary groups.

References

American Psychiatric Association (1994), *Diagnostic Criteria from DSM-IV*, American Psychiatric Association.

Attwood, T. (1998), *Asperger's Syndrome: A Guide for Parents and Practitioners,* London: Jessica Kingsley. Good standard text giving information on the disorder.

Clements, J. and Zarkowska, E. (2000), *Behavioural Concerns and Autism Spectrum Disorders: Explanations and Strategies for Change,* London: Jessica Kingsley.

Csoti, M. (1999*), People Skills for Young Adults,* London: Jessica Kingsley. Course in social skills training for teenagers; practical. Includes some role play and 'help sheets' for students.

Cumine, V., Leach, J. and Stevenson, G. (1998), *Asperger Syndrome: A Practical Guide for Teachers,* London: David Fulton. Aimed at school age but many ideas and strategies applicable to college students and their support workers. Includes 'top tips' for support staff.

Harrison, J. (1998), *Improving learning opportunities in mainstream secondary schools and colleges for students on the autistic spectrum,* British Journal of Special Education, **25**(4) 179–183.

Howlin, P. (1997), *Autism: Preparing for Adulthood,* London: Routledge. A must for the college learning support bookshelf.

Morgan, H. (1996), *Adults with Autism: a guide to theory and practice*, Cambridge: Cambridge University Press. Another good textbook for reference.

Powell, A. (2002), *Taking Responsibility: Good Practice Guidelines for services for adults with Asperger Syndrome,* The National Autistic Society.

Smith Myles, B. and Southwick, J. (1999), *Asperger Syndrome and Difficult Moments: Practical Solutions for Tantrums, Rages and Meltdowns,* distributed by Jessica Kingsley. The title says it all. Includes material about children and young people, lots of checklist, hints and ideas which can be adapted for college life.

Wing, L. (1988), *The continuum of autistic characteristics* in E. Schopler and G.B. Mesibov (Eds), *Diagnosis and Assessment in Autism,* New York: Plenum Press.

Wing, L. (1996) *The Autistic Spectrum: A Guide for Parents and Professionals,* London: Constable.

World Health Organisation (WHO) (1992), *The ICD-10 Classification of Mental and Behavioural Disorders,* Geneva: WHO.

Consider some texts written by those who have autism spectrum disorders:

Jolliffe, T. Lansdown, R. and Robinson, T. (1992), *Autism: A Personal Account,* London: The National Autistic Society.

Jackson, L. (2002), *Freaks, Geeks and Asperger Syndrome: A User Guide to Adolescence*, London: Jessica Kingsley.

Sainsbury, C. (2000), *Martian in the Playground*, Bristol: Lucky Duck Publishing. www.luckyduck.co.uk

Williams, D. (1996), *Autism: An Inside-Out Approach,* London: Jessica Kingsley. Her views on how autism affects the person's attempts to gain control over their life, with comments on others' approaches.

Williams, D. (1992, reprinted 1998), *Nobody Nowhere,* London: Jessica Kingsley. The first of her three autobiographies recounts her first 25 years.

Many of these books may be obtained from the National Autistic Society Publications. Tel: 0207 903 3595; email: publications@nas.org.uk or check the website www.nas.org.uk

Jessica Kingsley Publishers have a wide range of texts on autism spectrum disorders. View their website: www.jkp.com

View the David Fulton books through www.fultonbooks.co.uk

Winslow distribute a variety of books and programmes in language, social skills etc. Tel: 0845 921 1777.

Incentive Plus have materials on social skills, emotional literacy, behaviour skills. Tel: 01908 526 120; email: orders@incentiveplus.co.uk or view on www.incentiveplus.co.uk

Smallwood Publishing publish social skills materials. Tel: 01304 226900; www.smallwood.co.uk

For information on *Emotion Trainer*, contact Anna Masterman at Leeds Innovations. Tel: 0113 233 3444; www.emotiontrainer.co.uk

For information on *Mind Reading*, contact www.human-emotions.com or tel: 01845 130 6142.

Useful organisations

The **National Autistic Society** has a Helpline: 0870 600 8585. Join the NAS and receive a quarterly journal as well as news of workshops and conferences. Website: www.nas.org.uk

The society has lists of NAS centres for adolescents and adults.

The NAS has also produced a leaflet: *A GP's guide to adults with Asperger Syndrome.* This may also be helpful for college or university medical staff.

For respite and short breaks for those 16+ with ASD, try Autism Solutions. Tel: 01823 270384 or www.autismsolutions.co.uk

OAASIS is run by Lesley Durston and is part of the Hesley Group: it provides guidelines, training and advice to those caring for young people with autism spectrum disorders. Ask to go on the mailing list and receive news of courses, initiatives and details of their publications. Tel: 09068 633201 (60p a minute).

New Support Options, part of the New Dimensions Group Ltd, has charitable status. They work in partnership with several housing organisations to provide supported living services, packages of day care and community support services. In 2002 they were operating in parts of Berkshire, Hampshire, Oxfordshire and Surrey. Services are being developed in parts of Norfolk. Tel: 0118 929 7900; www.newsupport.org.uk

Hoffman de Visme Foundation is a registered charity providing counselling, outreach, consultation, assessments for adults with ASD. They can help with life skills, self-awareness and worth, management of anxiety, stress and depression. There is a charge for services that may be available from local Social Services or Primary Care Trusts or through the student's family GP. Tel: 0208 342 7316 for more information.

Berkshire Autistic Society (BAS) is a well-organised excellent local group: they have started a 19+ Support and Action Group to develop services in Berkshire: Contact BAS on tel: 0118 958 6022. This Society, funded by the local health and unitary authorities, conducted a major research project (1997–2000) to identify the needs of those with Asperger Syndrome in their area. Contact the society for an executive summary of the results by Sue Portway: there are useful pointers and recommendations for local services.

Autism West Midlands is another worthwhile group to contact: they have leaflets and guidelines. Contact them at 12 Oakfield Road, Selly Park, Birmingham B29 7EJ.

ASPEN (Asperger Syndrome Professional Network) is a group of professionals involved in developing services for those with Asperger Syndrome. They meet twice a year in London. You can find out more through the NAS website or by doing a search.

There are many useful websites. Use a well-established search engine to help (e.g. Lycos, Altavista, Google, Yahoo). Look for the 'advanced search' facility as this helps to narrow options for a specific topic. www.excite.com enables the user to search by category as well as key word, and www.hotbot.com is linked with Lycos to give double search chances.

www.udel.edu/bkirby/asperger puts the user in touch with OASIS: Online Asperger Syndrome Information and Support, an American organisation.

www.autism-society.org is the website of the Autism Society of America.

Appendix 1
Checklist for student entering college/university

Personal data:

- name, address, phone, email

- family input, who to best involve

- previous educational establishment/employment, contact details.

Support:

- did the students have support at school? (If yes, who, what, how often, in which subjects?)

- any special arrangements for SATs or GCSEs?

Reports to request:
(as relevant: not all students have Statements or SEN)

- copy of last Individual Education Plan

- statement of SEN

- last report by paediatrician/psychiatrist

- last report by speech and language therapist

- transitional review report.

Further relevant details:

- strengths and areas of success

- areas of difficulty (and in what circumstances)

- interests

- what resources were successful?

- what strategies were successful?

- what should staff avoid, if anything?

- on medication?

Personnel and permission to contact:

	Names	Contact details
Parents/carers		
GP		
Psychologist		
Psychiatrist/local child and adolescent services		
Social services		

Information on communication and social skills:

- following instructions (simple, several at once, oral, written)

- understanding non verbal gestures, cues and prompts

- how is the student in greetings, asking for help, turn taking, conversational repair, showing interest in others' conversations, ending a conversation, understanding jokes, labelling emotions, facial and body language, conveying messages?

- friends, social activities

- expressing emotions

- can convey message

- level of independence (travel, shops, handling money, around school, clubs)

- does the student know he/she has ASD, attitude

- skills in decision-making

- safety skills

- level of study skills: note taking, working independently, using texts as reference, where and how to gain help or information, organising study, timing written work

- sexual issues (knowledge, attitude, etc).

Behaviour:

- risk assessment.

Appendix 2
Individual Progress Plan

Some colleges use 'Learning Plan', 'Goals' or 'Course Plan' and it will be important for the student with autism spectrum disorder to follow the same system as other students with disabilities, providing the plan is full and detailed so that any member of staff looking at it would know how to help.

Include:

Name, course, tutor and support worker.

Target:

- Who will help deliver?

- When on timetable?

- Where (Room? Library? Canteen?)

- How will student be enabled?

- Type of help? (details of proximity of support worker, material resources, how often to intervene etc)

Date of review

Ensure student has copy of plan as well as key staff members. With the student's permission, give one to the parents/carers too so they can encourage, back up at home, etc.

Try to use coloured paper and stick to same colour so the plan is easily spotted in a folder, bag or on a desk.

Notes and helpful information
(for your own additons)